untreated

poems by black writers

compiled by josie douglas

D1707808

First published in 2001 by

jukurrpa books

an imprint of

IAD Press
PO Box 2531
Alice Springs
NT 0871

This work is copyright. Apart from any fair dealing for the purposes of private study, research, criticism or review, as permitted under the Copyright Act 1968, no part may be reproduced by any process without prior written permission. Please forward all inquiries to IAD Press at the address above.

Copyright in individual poems remains with the authors.
Copyright in this collection © IAD Press 2001.

Graeme Dixon's poem 'Darryl' first published in *Holocaust Island* (University of Queensland Press) 1990.
Kerry Reed-Gilbert's poem 'Let's Get Physical' first published in *Black Woman, Black Life* (Wakefield Press) 1996.
Rosemary Plummer's poems 'Silently' and 'Napanangka Has Gone Digging for Sand Frogs' first published in *Northern Perspective*, 1999 literary awards edition.

National Library of Australia Cataloguing-in-Publication data:

Untreated: poems by black writers.
ISBN 1 86465 039 7.
1. Australian poetry - Aboriginal authors. I. Douglas, Josie, 1970- .
A821.008089915

Design by Iben Hansen
Cover photograph by Mike Gillam
Printed in Australia by Hyde Park Press, Adelaide

Australia Council
for the Arts

This publication was assisted by the Federal Government through the Australia Council, its arts funding and advisory body.

Dedicated,
with respect,
to

Kevin Gilbert

Oodgeroo Noonuccal

Jack Davis

Contents

Foreword

Kim Scott

When I received this manuscript — *Untreated* — I tore the envelope open and immediately began skimming its pages. I was keen to see what it offered, and flattered to have been asked to write the foreword.

I recognised themes; history, injustice, identity, the desire to link our past and future, but what struck me — once again — was the diversity of forms our voices can take. I read poetry balanced by rhythm and rhyme; poetry that echoed, in its supple vocabulary, everyday speech; poetry powerfully petitioning the need for social change. And I read poetry that seemed like incantation, with its sense of springing from deep places, of being motivated by rhythms not offered this shape before, this guise of the English language.

Not all of the poetry in this collection is in English, certainly not 'standard' English. There's an example in an Indigenous language, and even in translation its restraint and control is poignant.

It's true, I think, that our Indigenous languages can be subtle and musical in a way for which English — that improvised stitching together of severed bits of various tongues — is too often barbaric and clumsy.

Often, but not always. The English used in this anthology is rarely clumsy. It is deftly deployed. Read these poems aloud. Listen.

It's not easy to say what 'poetry' is. Sometimes you hear it, sometimes you see it. It gives us, I think, a way of expressing what 'ordinary' language does not, cannot. 'Ordinary'

Australian English — and the ways of thinking it promotes — is often hostile to Indigenous Australia. Who among us can refuse the help, the hope and the healing, which poems can offer?

Reading this collection I was reminded that although many of us are not accepted for 'what we are' (to quote a mere half a line from this anthology), it's also true that *what we might be* is yet to be realised. Many of these poems help consolidate our pasts, and step toward a future. In diverse ways, together.

Our audience is also diverse. Some of the voices in this anthology address those on 'the fringes'. But after such an audience has respectfully listened, to what extent do they remain on the fringe? Doesn't this act of communication mean the 'fringe', the boundary, has begun to move outward?

There is regeneration, here in this book. Something is growing, and it grows from the Indigenous centres of these poets, their poems.

Christmas Dinner

Harold AhKup

We had Christmas in the bush that year,
potatoes, cornbeef and damper.
Wasn't much else we could do in the wet,
so that was our Christmas hamper.
Stinking heat and early rains
made work impossible on the blacksoil plains.
For the kids, no presents to be found;
trapdoor spiders in the ground;
together, we were all flood bound.

I'll never forget that year we had, Newbore and Gidyea Creek,
supper by the campfire, lit of a yellow moon;
listen to a dingo's howl
way down, at Palmers Lagoon.

Greying hair and fading eyes,
potguts and lazy style.
A crowbar weighs a ton these days,
... can't use a pair of pliers.

Hot days, and cold nights,
those days long ago I'll remember.
A plague of rats and locusts,
and a very wet December.

Floating logs and crawling snakes,
enough to make you shiver,
but a great sight, a must to see,
is the swollen Curry River.

Through rain and mud, and spirits high,
our sis stood out the winner.
Walk backwards to Bourke,
you'll never find
no finer Christmas dinner.

Old Blue 'the cook'

Harold AhKup

Hey Blue, what's for supper t'night?
I suppose it's cornbeef stew,
ah well, it'll be better than ya custard mate,
that tastes a bit like glue.

What did we eat last night ol' Blue?
Was it kind of mashed potato,
I weren't game ta ask, it coulda bin Uncle Toby's Oats,
or a pot of gooey sago.

Ah, old Blue's not a bad old cook,
who else could burn the brew?
He'd be a whole lot better tho,
than some cleanskin jackeroo.

No one wants that bloody job,
'til old Blue said he could cook,
he said he cooked on Bulla-Roo,
but I coulda bin mistook.

We'll have ta grin an bear it,
whatever old Blue cooks.
When the mailman comes around next week,
we'll get some posh cook books.

But who wants ta eat filet mignon,
prepared by our ol' cook, Blue?
It wouldn't be the bloody same,
I'd prefer his cornbeef stew.

A Significant Life

Lisa Bellear

A life story, my history placed
within artificial boundaries of colonial
discourse. Hey what do these hackademics
anthros, researchers, archivists want
for nothing?

Authorisation is signed. The standard ethics
agreement between researcher and subject
is politely referred to. Tape recorder is
switched on. How difficult for me to recall
events of social, cultural and political
significance.

Memories bring on overwhelming grief.
Yet we sit drinking sugary tea discussing
a life which is no more or less significant
or distinguishable from others who have
survived to this point.

For the future I release this silenced
voice. For the future I will go beyond
my hidden pain and expose a snapshot
insight into an urban/rural Indigenous
survivor. For the future, if there is to be one,
we must listen, talk and share. For the future.

Love's Polished Floor

Lisa Bellear

Cold isolated scary deep
coloured abstract art
violent helpless dirt poor
raw emotions. The worst
punch was the first.

Scrumpled into an invisible
heap. Cornered on the recently
polished blak and white
linoleum.

A knock on the door.
Paralysed — waiting — simpering
in silence. Thwack. A louder
knock, two authoritative voices.
Her heartbeat is thumping
thumping, thumping.

No way out.

Genocide

Lisa Bellear

Laws what laws there are
no laws that define
articulate elucidate validate
GENOCIDE

Australia conveniently will
not initiate and legislate laws
based on genocide

Through the valiant efforts
of our warriors without
treaties genocide will
be validated in law your
federated Australia!

Intimations of a CVA

John Muk Muk Burke

The veins of my nicotine hands stand out
So I know my brain's all right.
The tightness in my skin
Is from thin brown whisky
Which my mate and I
Drank late into the night
With arm wrestling.
Testing one another
Tightly loving one another
Real mates,
Kissing hands.
Not thinking of tomorrow
And that which must yet come
At the heart of things
From too much wrestling
In this world.

The Builder

John Muk Muk Burke

I see a tattooed arm
Inside the window
Lifted to the sun,
To the crane lowering the roof.
Hairs glowing, muscles moving
A slow wind over water,
Brown
Holding up
His workman's pannikin
Pouring liquid down his throat
Like Uriah
With his check shirt tossed
Across the scaffold.

He rolls a smoke and turns,
Turns, turns —
Shoulders moving
Through the soft white cloud
He breathes
Into
The incomplete abode.
And the good Earth turns, turns, turns
With its labouring human load.

Darryl

Graeme Dixon

Though the town's forgotten
I remember well
a skinny half-caste kid
hanging in a cell
Your body was caught
in the pain of life
and the agonised throes
of violent strife
We were all stunned
with terror and fear
those of us left who loved you so dear
There will never ever
be time to forget
your agonised face
and that leather boot lace
They cut your shell down
gave it respect
more than they gave you in life
when proudly erect
But you were a child
a product of time
a little bit lost
a little bit wild

Loving and gently,
slightly uncouth
they refused you the right
to outgrow your youth
But I remember you Darryl
your humour your smile
the good times we shared
for a space and a while
And sometimes when I'm down
and alone in the night
I wonder what would have been
had they treated you right
If you were alive
you would be thirty today
maybe contentedly watching
your children at play.

Friday Night in Hell

Graeme Dixon

Obese barman bellows
'Time for last drinks!'
Young, angry blackfellows
Kick up a stink
A pool stick is broken
As sparked temper flares
Shirts sweat soaked
Piercing blood-shot stares

Sparkling golden beer
Splashed with scarlet blood
A threatening dropped lip sneer
From yesterday's stud
Who throws a clumsy jab
Clipping burly bouncer's ears
Knife appears — stabs!
Blood flows like tears

Again it's drunken brawling
At the Railway Hotel
Punch drunk dancing
To the jukebox bell
Batons at the ready
Police arrive to quell

Splitting drunken heads
On this Friday night in hell

Into meat vans
Toss the walking and lame
Arrest all you can
They all look the fucking same

If they resist
Bash 'em to the ground
Skull baton-kissed
Sickening cracking sound

Frightened girl cries out
'Leave my man alone!'
Loser of the bout
In his blood lies prone
'Get an ambulance!'
An anxious brother calls
But they couldn't care less
— they are the law

Police rev engines
Screech for lock-up cells
Ignorant of their sins
On this Friday night
In hell

Farewell Charlie

Graeme Dixon

That fighting spirit from freedom rides
has sadly passed on by
That fair bastard like you and I
has gone to stir up the vast blue sky
Or maybe take some precious time
to play soccer in the bye and bye
Maybe rest for a little while
but still wearing that cheeky smile
That sometimes made one believe
others took him more serious than he
He who loved to agitate
some people loved, others loved to hate
But none could ever take away
his right to stand and have his say
about injustice's burdening down
or chained his people to the ground
Yes, that spirit from freedom rides
has sadly passed on by
That fair bastard like you and I
has gone to stir up the bye and bye
That fair bastard like you and I
has gone to stir up the bye and bye
Please welcome him gods, he has earned his reprise

R.I.P. Charles Perkins

Fire in Our Bellies

Jim Everett

We all sat round listenin' t' them two coes
Blackfellas ours, but government fullas
They was sayin' how we had no choice
Take th' government deal at Preminghana
Or don't get no land back
The talk was about the road up there
They want t' put a road across our land
Across our heritage at Preminghana
And these government blackfellas
Were pushin' the bosses line real solid
One government blackfella got huffy
When we told him he *was* government
But we all knew it was the government's land council
This statutory agency under the minister
So the argument changed an' we told 'em
You go back to yuh boss an' tell 'im
We've given up too much already
It's our land an' we fought hard for it
Right through the seventies and eighties

With fire in our bellies
An' we still got that fire

So you go back t' your white boss

An' you tell 'im bro's
We give up too much already
An' it's time for whites to give way

We could feel the fire in our bellies
Once again.

*Preminghana (Mount Cameron West — north-west coast of
Tasmania)*

16

Our Earth Eyes

Jim Everett

We see your paper mills
Woodchip piles and smoking stacks
We see Mount Fuji
In the haze of industry
We met those people of the market
They who buy our forests free
Who speak of good in double tongue
We came from Tasmania to see
With our Earth Family
Where our forests are chewed
And paper rolled for throw-aways
We looked in your country
Where tradition on land
On bended knee holds sway
Against big paper makers
And pray that like cherry blossom
They will come and go
Yet like our forests free
That are clear felled down
And pray
That they the paper makers
Of our woodchipped trees
Will not return.

Two World One

Richard Frankland

I'm a two world one
I live in two worlds
One time I must have lived in one

But tears fell and a baby taken
Under some law they said
A law from one world but not the other

I'm a two world one
I walk down two roads
One time I must have only walked down one

But surely a mother's heart was broken
At a birthing tree or birthing room
When I was taken

I'm a two family one
I live with two families
One is black one is white

But surely heritage is no barrier to love
Even though the papers scream
About the two hundred years of hurt and shame

I'm a two world one
I can see inside two worlds
But one day I'll only have to see in one

Uncle

Richard Frankland

Oh Uncle
I did it
because
When I woke up in gaol
I looked
to my future and seen
Me getting drunk again
fighting again
Getting stoned again
Hating myself again
Stealing again
Hurting people again
Getting locked up again
And Uncle I didn't like it
Cause when I woke up
I looked
to my future
And I didn't have one
That's why Uncle
That's why
I tried to die

A New Day Dawning

Richard Frankland

There is a new day dawning
I am sure, I am sure
Where everyone will see only love
And hatred will be no more
There is a change that is coming
I am sure, I am sure
Where differences will be celebrated
The end of religions and war
Where money will not be the price of land
And heaven will be where we stand
And elders will be elders
Like it was before
There is a new day dawning
I am sure, I am sure

Camellia Law

Mary Graham

The flowers, Camellias I think they were, said to John
Look, we can help you with this workshop,
Why don't you place us on the low table in the centre of the
    group and ask everyone to comment on our presence?
We're used to modeling and displays and exhibitions.

Happiness and wonder dance around the room
Silence and reflection take small stately steps.

From ancient Chinese paintings to dry Canberra gardens,
    Camellias know, too, that the Law moves in mysterious
    ways.

White and Black poetry readings: distinct differences

Anita Heiss

Jatz Crackers, block cheese and chardonnay sipping
      Politics, emotions and conscience ripping

Big words to aid the mental masturbation
      Simple message: Aboriginal incarceration

Autumn leaves falling from age-old trees
      Begging for human rights on bended knee

The blackness of night and stars so bright
      Chanting for basic human rights

Judging all those who dwell beneath
      Laying another black death in custody wreath

Analysing another famous sporting broadcast
      Denying emphatically Truganini was the last

Middle class life where the Volvo is vital
      Why are we still fighting for Native Title?

I'm a vegan, against anything meaty
      I want sovereignty and a treaty

Worrying about the lack of sexual stimulation
    Telling the truth of the Stolen Generations

Mixing with the best at the City's town hall
    Tired of being the political football

The colour has contrast, context and depth
    I'll be black till my dying breath

I'm not racist, a bigot or bum
    I'm still trying to find my mum

I've done my bit for reconciliation
    While I'm still begging for self-determination

The new tax reform is the country's biggest worry
    But we're still campaigning for Howard's 'Sorry'

There is no difference between you and me
    Except that you write from a position of being free.

enough

sammy howard

to watch our people too frightened to say
we are what we are accept us that way
enough is enough
to be told we are not, and if we are only half
nowhere to go to have as our own
enough is enough
if we don't make a stand all will be lost
if it were theirs their cry would be heard
enough is enough
we've stood and watched as time has gone by
the destruction of our shrines for science and mankind
enough is enough
as the spirits watch us with wide furrowed brows
can we unite to continue the fight
enough is enough
our time has come to unite as one
to hold all those dear and make our stand clear
when will we finally say
we have had enough

Between Two Worlds

Terri Janke

Back to the world I live in
Clean white men in drycleaned suits
blue white collars concealing thick necks
dark shoes with clean soles
clean fingernails, manicured
Preened greying hair
Black slimline mobile phones like head mutations talking
clinching that deal
talking loud enough so that everyone can overhear
and understand that they are important.

As I stare down at the striped carpet of the airport
I am invisible
I am the night
Dark corners unfolding
Passing unnoticed
or as jigsaw fragments of an exotic erotica
When did the girl become the woman
The trap is laid bare
There is distinct passion in my step
I am resilient
As I slide to cover your weakness.

I am the ocean

A timeless hereditary spirit

My dark ancestors lay a silver blanket over me

In the moonlight, but in life they had nothing to give

Nothing that was not already taken

The last time they slept on the sand

The last time I stepped off a plane.

Journey

Terri Janke

Descent in flight
The wing cut through the streaky white
As a sliver of sunlight reflected against metal.
Abundant greenness covered the mountains and clouds,
Thick and wet, clung to the peaks.

Islands, white sand, mangroves, green blue water tossed with
    white foam
And then sugar fields, red dirt, houses, buildings,
Yachts at the harbour
And the esplanade with Cairns Base Hospital, where I was
    born.

On the melting tarmac
I inhaled the earth
I took in the humidity
I missed this place.

Mentors

Terri Janke

Our mentors are our mothers, our fathers,
Our families, our ancestors.
The people we love.
The people who gave us breath.
Our places, our lands,
Our homes, our ways —
The features that make us unique.

The Gubberments

Ruby Langford Ginibi

When whiteman bin commin alonga this way
Aboriginal people had no place left ta stay
gone was our tucker, emu and roo
run from the fences the whiteman he knew.
That's what is gubberment tellem ta do
puttem all on mission, that's where they all should be
gibem white manager e tellem what ta do.
Gotta stay on mission ground
neber wander all ober town
I gibe you all rations ta lubra and kids
ya gotta work for tucker ya git
missionary come he teach us 'lidgen
ya gotta be good ta go ta heben.
They always tellen us what ta do!
Like we got nothin ta thinkem with too
then they takem away our kids they'll be back one day!
our mother and father have nothin ta say
trooper and mission truck him bin takem away
and we neber seen em for many a day
some kids they bin neber come ome again
why whiteman cause so much pain?

Black Woman

Ruby Langford Ginibi

I am every black woman who's ever been in love.

I am every black woman who's been serenaded by a guitar on
a starry night.

I am every black woman who's ever been betrayed by a selfish
lover.

I am every black woman who's given birth to loved children.

I am every black woman who's had to work on fence lines, to
raise them too!

I am every black woman who's hungered after truth.

I am every black woman who's ever carted water buckets on
yokes to fill a forty-four gallon drum for drinkin, washin,
and cookin purposes.

I am every black woman who's had a son or husband jailed.

I am every black woman who's had iron doors slammed shut
going to visit them too!

I am every black woman who's struggled to raise a fine.

I am every black woman whose heart has been broken over
the deaths of loved ones.

I am every black woman who has survived this calamity
we call life, in this now multicultural Australia!

Agony

Kenny Laughton

This storm keeps rolling around in my head
Sometimes I don't care if I am alive or dead
Laying here in my sleepless bed
Sweating and shaking, that feeling of dread
Why is it still here after all these years?
Try as I may I can't hold back the tears
I get so frustrated I want to scream and shout
'What the fuck is this all about?'
The scars are invisible but they are there
Is there anyone out there who really cares?
It's a long hard road and I wonder if I'll make it?
A lot of my mates sure couldn't take it
Snuffed themselves out well before their time
Have the 'experts' learnt anything from what they left
    behind?
I beg the question, 'When will it all end?'
Maybe death will be my only friend.

My Special Place

Kenny Laughton

My mind's eye
It looks out for me
There's no prejudice there
It's full of good memories
Like a cave
Washed with paintings and stories
Impressions of my life
When times get tough
I dig deep within myself
Found that inner strength
That self-being that is me
Not sad but enduring
Comforting
My mind's eye
Is my special place
No one can hurt me there

You Are the Fringes

Melissa Lucashenko

If you go over the red roads to that country
people might look at your government toyota.
Black faces clouded by life in the sunlit dust
will glance up and in one fast summary sweep know you:
you are the fringes.

> Standing in the silence at Kata Tjuta a slow plane didjeridoos
>   its way
> Across a high high sky.
> There is little to say about such a place.
> If I was to speak, my words would carry in them the legends
>   of Fence,
> Wall, House, City, Thief, stranger ... my words are not good
>   currency here.

Back in town German tourists browse neon dot-art, looking for
Australopithicas.
The media curses euphemistic drunks in the mall, and caught
    between,
hopeful, sympathetic, informed, you wander to the river edge,
where shaggy gums bend to caress the campers.

(Did you sit in the sand there? Did you drink, or leave your
    spawn?

Did you sit and wonder there? Or was your whiteness
    scorned?)
Whichever you remember, whichever way it was,
The campers still are real there, their sites are talking all the
    day now,
and you ... *you are the fringes*.

Those first whites, human or ghostspirits, came talking of
    something bigger than economics.
Came with missions and belief, but later, despite all available
    evidence,
refused faith in any but themselves.
You said savages and humpies; you said All God's Children.
You said come walk beside us, our little black selves from
    another time.
You even said sorry.
It matters little. Words are noise in a desert of silence.
When will you learn?
You: you are the fringes.

I Am Not My Life

Melissa Lucashenko

Sue-Ann her leg it long and brown, her arm it needle-thin.
Her dark dark eye betray the lie, the look, the hand between
   the thigh,
The neverending woman trial to get the money in.
To get the cash to make the dash
To sink into her skin.

Sue-Ann her hair it long and brown, she young, she sweet,
   she wear a crown
of beauty that the man all hound,
Him hungry eye can drag you down, can drag and tear you to
   the ground
Before he sneer and grin.
And then the paper in you hand, it far too late to take a
   stand,
And this the way that things have panned, cos Sue-Ann's on
   again.
She on the gear again.

Sue-Ann she on a course these days, her eye it full of sun.
The Gubbas pay to let her dream of fame and fortune, life
   unseamed,
Her life of welfare seem so lean,

But camera eye he not so keen, can't see the blood, can't see
    how mean
The street to young Sue-Ann have been.
Sue-Ann she write, Sue-Ann she speak, she be the woman
    she will be,
We wait, and wonder silently and never know what we might
    see,
She on the gear again, think we, she on the gear again.

She young, she sweet, she wear a crown,
She look so scorn at all around,
Sue-Ann ain't lost, Sue-Ann ain't found,
She on the gear again, that all, she on the gear again.
The family sigh, avoid her eye, her mumma she lean back and
    cry,
She on the gear again, that girl, she on the stuff again.

The Work Ethic

Melissa Lucashenko

Bigcity

Buses stop, offload their stumbling, besuited contents.

The carpark fills, early morning trips to the airport are made,

hotels reserved, breakfasts consumed, flex sheets annotated

    in ever more flexible fashions.

The modern grey building bides its time.

Its morning meal of bureaucrats never wanes, they will

    always come to answer

the patience of the bricks and steel.

Here we are, as bidden, we walk, fly, crawl to work,

Hating every minute, resenting the seconds of stolen life, the

slatternly way this animal tosses our souls to deputised lions.

Blacktown

Meanwhile, back at the ranch:

Jacky sits and smokes, hardly listens anymore to the children

    screaming.

His sister is working in the Council office and will buy a new

    toyota soon,

A four wheel drive for hunting; Jacky will be a man again

    when this happens.

Jacky dreams of a new gun, of swiftly snatched perentie on

    the fire ...

His brother stirs, walks carelessly to the wet canteen for ten
o'clock opening.
Mary nurses last night's bruises, eager for Ray Martin to come
and take the pain away.
Teenagers ride motorbikes through the town, past the petrol
cages, past the store,
leaving in the swirling dust behind them
every blow, every curse, every ugly thing that ever happened
here.

Aunt Dolly is painting again. Her picture will tell the tourists
about when Jesus came to Blacktown.
Here is Jesus. His work is to hang on a cross, promising
salvation.
Here is the whiteman. His work is to tell Jacky things, and
frown, and write in his big book.
Here is Mary. Her work is to have brown babies, and cook,
and wash the mission floors.

Here are the children, look now — their work is to be hungry
and sick
for the sad white people,
and also for the black people who shout at the white people.
Here is Jacky, his work is pretending to be happy.

Justice Being Denied

June Mills

Black man hangs from a rope, he didn't deserve to die
people say it was suicide, but justice has been denied
baby taken from its mother's arms, never to be seen again
mother cries herself to death, justice has been denied

Whiteman steals a black man's land, and claims it for his own
black man claims his sovereignty, but justice is being denied
a young girl lies in her bed, her brain has been long dead
just a victim of society, because justice is being denied

She said rose oil allows for anger release

Romaine Moreton

Allure fading like the dusk,
rocking between solace and seldom despair,
she noticed the daffodils were in full bloom,
quite early for this time of year.

Many ordinary women pondered the curse of beauty,
and the unrequited attention it attracts,
fondling the dilemma of being loved simply
for the sake of beauty itself.

She cupped the bulb of a daffodil
in her wrinkled shrivelling hand
and wondered what life would have been like
had others thought her smart.

I Shall Surprise You By My Will

Romaine Moreton

I will make oppression work for me,
With a turn and with a twist,
Be camouflaged within stated ignorance,
Then rise,
And surprise you by my will,

I will let you pass me over,
Believe me stupid and ill informed,
And once you believe me gone or controlled
Will rise
And surprise you by my will,

I shall spring upon you words familiar,
Then watch you re-gather as they drop about,
Like precious tears thick with fear,
Hear you scream and shout,
Then I shall watch convictions break away,
And crumple like paper bags,
And then as beauty I shall rise,
And surprise you by my will,

It is only when you believe me gone,
Shall I rise,
From this place where I

Wait
Cross legged
Wait,
To surprise you by my will,

In the alleys, in the clubs, in the parliaments,
In courts of law, parking cars, driving buses,
And generally watching you
Watching me
As you pass me by,

I shall wait cross legged
Wait,
To surprise you by my will,

For I shall stumble from houses of education,
And I shall stumble from institutions of reform,
I shall stumble,
Over rocks, over men, over women, and over children,
And surprise you by my will,

I shall stumble over poverty, over policies, and over prejudice,
Weary and torn,
I stumble,
Then bleary and worn I shall rise,
From this place where I wait cross legged,
Wait,

And surprise you by my will,

For the mountains we crossed,
They were easy,
And the rivers we swam,
They were easier still,
And even then,
As I attempted to outrun inhumanity,
I surprised you by my will,

I have witnessed the falling of many,
Heard them cry and hear them still,
Even with grief inside me growing,
I command my spirit to rise,
And surprise you by my will,

And for all people,
We are here and we are many,
And we shall surprise you by our will,
We shall rise from this place where you expect
To keep us down,
And we shall surprise you by our will,

For the bullets we dodged,
They were difficult,
And this ideological warfare
More difficult still,

But even now,
As we challenge inhumanity,
We shall rise,
And surprise you by our will.

Soap is Easy

Romaine Moreton

The white woman come up to her and say,
'Hello Siss'

She blacker than me black girl thought,
'cause she know all them black fella words
all them black fella lingo
all them black fella things,

While she,
who hardly knew her own black skin,
didn't know them black fella idiom
them black fella things,

The white woman went to shop: needed soap,
and being justifiably pecuniary,
bought it,
To wash her lily white skin
Her lily white sin

Cause sometimes she felt bad,
felt guilty,
For the true history she knew;

and soap was easy,

Black woman needed material sympathy,
and being justifiably pecuniary,
bought a dress,
To cover her dark skin
Her dyed in the dark sin,

Cause sometimes she felt bad,
felt guilty,
As her true identity she didn't know,

then dress up was easy.

The Rule of Bread

Bruce Pascoe

No pretext exists for the cessation of war
the United Nations has declared,
indeed all perfidy may continue as before,
except that the rule of bread is absolute.

Any soldier of any nation for any reason
may kill another being whether man, woman, or child
of any race or religion
at any time, in any way
while the rule of bread is observed.

The soldier gives the insurgent, traitor, infidel, heathen,
oil baron, border-crosser, secret stealer, fifth columnist,
unemployed, political demonstrator or vagrant
a loaf of bread,
inviting the accused to eat the loaf, the whole loaf,
and nothing but the loaf.

Upon the expiry of the three days it takes to consume the
    loaf,
and some prisoners have been known to take ten or more,
if at that time the soldier continues to feel the same anger,
his knowledge of the prisoner's crimes remains as certain as
    before,

or he has not thrown a stick for the prisoner's dog,
married his sister, borrowed a pair of pants from his father,
learnt to respect his mother,
become fond of the curried chicken of his aunt,
or indeed, lost complete interest and gone home to mow the
    lawn,
he may shoot the prisoner,
no questions asked.

There will be, from hereon, no restriction on the conduct of
    war
or the level of violence delivered,
other than the observance of the rule of bread.
Bon appetit, my brothers.

Napanangka Has Gone Digging for Sand Frogs

Rosemary Plummer

Napanangka had gone digging for sand frogs
She wakes up
and crawls out of her humpy
made out of old blankets and sheets of iron
She yawns
and speak
'It is a beautiful day
the rain has stopped
I'll go digging for sand frogs
It's my favourite food'
She stretch her right hand, picked
her digging stick and small coolamon
from top of the humpy
then call out to other
women who lived nearby her
'I'm going
out to get sand frogs'

'Good' they replied
who had all return
their request to bring
back some

She wandered off
singing ten pella-iiiiiii
or twenty pella-iiiiiii

The sky looked grey
yet more rain
expected according
to other women

Along the yellow
spinifex, tiny raindrops
left from the last shower
but nothing worried
Napanangka

Meanwhile, back
at the camp
other women prepared
their humpies, fixing holes
putting over old blankets, sheet of iron
also collect wood
making sure
they had plenty to
keep them warm
during the wet weather

Eagerly fading, alone,

into the bush
Napanangka stop and said to herself
'My goodness it's unnecessary
to stay. All I'm wanting
is to have sand frogs for
my tea. Those women are crazy
they too should have come'.

She walked a fair way
Passing through high spinifex
small scrub
on a damp ground

Finally she made it
with amazement
she came upon a
sandhill where sand frogs'
holes were
(sand frogs can survive in all seasons)
How she find the sand frogs
She looked for the dirt
rising about three inches
top of the ground surface

Napanangka dug one hole
Without hesitation she began digging
nearly two hours

using her digging stick, small
coolamon to help throw dirt out

She dug at least six feet down
and about three feet
across

Having found one
she pinched inside its nose (stop from breathing)
threw it
on the ground
repeating, kept finding
four to six until coming
to the bottom
where she find lots of big brown sand frogs (about fifty)
all on top of themselves

Napanangka was thrilled
she kill all of them
by twisting their noses
one by one and
threw them on the ground
When she finish killing them all
she put some dirt
on the coolamon
then put all the frogs
onto the coolamon

using some dirt to cover
(to keep it fresh and from flies)

'This is plenty' she said 'Enough
Now I will be able to share'.

She pick her coolamon
with frogs in it, digging stick,
made her way back using the same footpath
through spinifex small scrub
on a damp ground

Coming close to the camp
late in the afternoon
she saw
other women have
already made a fire
knowing Napanangka would bring sand frogs

They were pleased
To see Napanangka
with lot of sand frogs

Everyone helped in cooking
Firstly they threw frogs onto
the charcoal
to get rid of sticky skin
when finished they buried

them under hot ashes and
waited fifteen minutes
to cook

When the frogs were cooked
the women got them out
of the hot ashes and
put them back onto the coolamon
They all find a
space to sit
and share the frogs

Carefully they split the stomach open
with their fingers and
took out intestine and the liver
They ate the liver first
Secondly enjoying the frog
for their main meal

All of the women praised Napanangka
being a good hunter and digger
of sand frogs

Silently

Rosemary Plummer

Not a wind
nor air we wait silently for
our spirit to tell our body had been
healed we wait patiently for the circulation
of the weather and the right time to gather bush
potatoes no sound of snake hissing in the grass we
wait for the rain wait and wait a bush fire burns the
ashes fall the fire leaves no track the root of a tree does
not exist any more a new tree must grow a new life start
how long now it gotta heal up I hear a voice must be must
be far away we paint our bodies now preparing to dance a
whirly wind swirl and swirl leaving broken branches and
leaves it makes the heart pound like the clock long time
now long time but we'll wait and wait just like a mother
giving birth to a new born baby I see the stars above at
night wonderful a silent river flows makes our spirit
inside of us calm so we'll wait silently patiently
for our spirit to tell us our body had been
healed and for the right time for the
circulation of the weather no
preparation to dance but
to wait wait wait

Words Are History

Boori Monty Pryor

Invasion
Oops!
That word sounds so intrusive
And not inclusive
At all
Oh
You'll settle for settle
ok
I'm sorry

Rape!
Oops!
That's such a nasty word
Oh
You've heard
So there was no intent
Just love and consent
ok
I'm sorry

Genocide
Oops!
Now there's a word for the ages
One you'll never find in the history pages
Oh

It was smallpox then
Aah, so that's when
They all died of misadventure
ok
I'm sorry

Stolen generations
Oops!
Now these two words are hard to separate
Just like a mother and child
Oh
It's all there in black and white
Right
The children were made with consent
But were taken away for their own good
Aah, now it's understood
There wasn't enough of them taken away
To constitute a generation
ok
I'm sorry

Fault!
Oops!
Where there's fault, there's blame
And what's in a name
'It's not my fault, wasn't even there'
That's fair
But you are here now

Oh
That's for someone else to do
Not you
ok
I'm sorry but I have to tell you
That invasion, rape, genocide, stolen generation and fault
Are not words shrouded in mystery
They are all part of our history
I know you probably can't see them
But I can read them, because I bleed them
Every day

Heartbeat

Boori Monty Pryor

In a heartbeat,
if I could
I would
take your place my sisters

In a heartbeat,
if I could
I would
die for you my brothers

In a heartbeat,
if I could
I would
take your pain away my nephew

In a heartbeat
if I could
I would
give and do all these things
just to hear your heart beat
again

Let's Get Physical

Kerry Reed-Gilbert

Let's get physical
The man cried, five in the morning
They lined up side-by-side row-by-row

Let's get physical
The boss man cried as he started them off
On their walk for miles

In between rows they did walk
Backs bent, too tired to talk

Let's get physical
The white man cried as he watched them
Pick his cotton, make his money
To put in his bank

Let's get physical
The white man cried, he'll never know
The Koori pride that makes that man
Bend between his rows

Koori pride is what it is
That makes that Black man
Bend his back, to pick his cotton
To pay his rent, to feed his kids

Welfare checks not for him
A honest day work says he'll win
Kids' belly full that's all that matters

Let's get physical
The white man cried he doesn't look
To see the pride in the Black man's eyes

Bindimayi's song about country

Translated by Peter Stevens and Nelson Hughes

Martanga-ullu-la tharkiart marna kuwarnha-la putarri
Kulawina yarku kujurri kuralanha

When I come back to my country,
Someone has built a stockyard on the flat land,
And a whitefella, Bluey, is sleeping in my birthplace.

* Guruma language, from the Pilbara region of Western Australia

Nguwarri Minyma
(Pretty Woman)
Alf Taylor

You are a

Nguwarri Minyma

Nguwarriest Minyma

I ever seen

Not in movies

Television

Or glamour

Books

But a

Nguwarri Minyma

In a community

Next to

Desert sand.

How

You took me

By the hand

Led me

Through that

Dry spinifex

Land

And how

We loved

On that

Warm evening

Desert sand

Indeed

You are

Nguwarri Minyma.

Didjeridoo and Clapsticks

Alf Taylor

As a child
In a mission
I heard the sounds
So far away
Sounds of the
Didjeridoo and clapsticks
Together
Rustling the tips
Of my mind
As I dream
I see
The red and white
Ochre figures
Dance before me

With the
Stamping of feet
On the ground
Slowly the dust
Rises
By a warm
Glowing firelight
I want

This dream
To stay
With me
All night

Not the
Morning
Prayers, school
Jesus
And floggings
I want
But the
Beautiful sounds
Of the
Didjeridoo and clapsticks
Forever
In my heart
And soul

The Frog-mouth Owls and the Cork Tree

Pat Mamanyjun Torres

When I was young in Broome, a favourite place
    to be,
Was standing near McDaniels corner under the
    old cork tree.
Two tiny frog-mouth owls could always be
    found there,
And many a child would throw a stone without
    a single care.

This act wasn't just a childhood idea of fun,
But done because the tree and owl were
    believed to be from Satan.
The stories about Ngardi the devil, the frog-
    mouth owls and the cork tree,
Is an old belief passed down from the people
    of Yawuru and Garajari.

I remember many a picture show and basketball night
Running past that dreadful tree in such a terrible fright
Cause many a strange sight could be seen by all
Like small cats and dogs with bright red eyes that grew and
    grew so tall.

Today we still believe in our family

That frog-mouth owls and cork trees are bad luck you see

And if one lands real close to us

We run out shouting and creating such a fuss

To scare away this symbol of evil

Cause no-one wants to be around the devil.

In Broome today the old cork tree and its owls are no longer
    to be seen

And only my memories remain to tell of the sights I've seen.

Milangka

Pat Mamanyjun Torres

Before her birth, in my dream I came to see,
A large Nimanburr, the flying fox hanging in a
    giant boab tree,
And then at once before my eyes a small dark
    child with curly hair,
Did laugh and somersault into the air,
She turned but once and stood up tall,
Her gaze so strong and her body small,
She looked up towards me smiling all the while,
I knew at once that I was to be the mother of
    this little dream child,
I felt all warm and funny inside,
My heart full of love and my mind full of pride.
How lucky I felt to be chosen by you,
To be your mother all our life through,
My first-born I promise to love and care for you
    as best I can,
And teach you the right and wrongs of life's
    great plan.

* Dedicated to my first-born, Emmanuelle Torres, whose bush name is Milangka.

Rain-making at Beagle Bay

Pat Mamanyjun Torres

Back in my old gran's day,
At Beagle Bay,
The old people had a way,
Of making rain, they say.

The people would sit with folded arms and
    head held high,
Then a few fluffy clouds would slowly pass by,
All would think of lightning and rain and stare
    to the sky,
But run and scatter when the lightning flashed
    and the rain fell, stinging into their eye.

the night house

Samuel Wagan Watson

the dingles of branches paint the night house
while the smoky residue left by the hate of its past
changes the degrees of shadow
                    from black to red

as if Dante himself
had tattooed the evicted limbs of humanity who had come
        here to lounge
as urban myth also dictates
that once-upon-a-time
                    black women had their babies in this yard
before the bulldozers mowed down the birthing plain
and erected the doomed foundations of the night house
                                unable to stop
                                        the curses falling

the lips of primal vengeance
camouflaged with an eternal apron of midnight's plague,

and just what is left, after night has devoured it?

it is not the smell of Sunday roast that lingers in the air
but other fleshes that purge
from the night house,

and the crows that cackle in its unkept grounds
that they too have witnessed the decrepitude
and the shallowness of love
as the trail leading to the front door
is the sinewy line between life and death
and burdening tales of woe,
the inhabitants always wondering,
why nothing has gone right here
and just how the walls manage to stay upright?

old dishes under the verandah
where man once tended the beast
as in the wind rattles an abandoned dog chain
now a resident umbilical to the nerve agents
that impregnate the unsoiled dreams of children
who play in the street by its wake,
whilst the demons clear the longevity of this place
and all the other night houses
built amidst atrocities and actions,

the consummate icons of irreversible history,

the sepia images of painful memory
    that form the blackening fringes of this sun-burnt country

Untitled

Samuel Wagan Watson

fire-engine-flash of fox pelt
and a plume of tail
fluffy ... like some oil well ablaze on a Gulf War postcard
and from the body
it was fleeing at a 2 o'clock incline

almost innocent in the ebb of dawn
above the vineyards at Booranga
sauntering erratically
as if it were copying the destiny of a red beacon
across the screen of a life-support monitor

up and down and away
                    this alien enigma upon Wiradjuri skin

She Spoke in Tongue

Brenda Webb

She glided past on the motion of the river
Her black hair plastered to her face from the wind
Her slender hand pulled strands of hair from her lips
She spoke in tongue
Sweet sounds dripping from her mouth
caressing my ears
comforting my soul
She was gone as quick as she came

Something Else

Brenda Webb

Sydney — having coffee before I went into court in support
    of a friend of mine.

This guy had just got out of jail the day before and he was
    wearing a borrowed suit too big for his size, runners & a
    $29 tie he had bought for $2 at an op shop.

The other boys were saying how he could sing & play guitar.

He was saying he was real proud of himself 'cause I'm off the
    gear and I don't rely on no 'done.'

He had olive skin & familiar eyes.

He was charged with conspiracy.
He sang opera and he sang fucking well.

When I asked if he was a blackfella
he said his mother was English and his father
was something else.

He sure looked like a brother to me.

Contributors

Harold AhKup was born in 1934 to John and Dolly AhKup on Lawn Hill Station, on a selection called Louie Creek, where his grandparents Sam and Opal AhBow had a market garden. They supplied the station and surrounding properties with fresh vegetables. When Harold's grandfather died he was buried on the property. Shortly after, his family moved to Cloncurry and they all grew up there.

Harold worked at various occupations in the bush, until he commenced work for the Mt Isa Mines in 1958. In 1961 he married and reared four children. Harold now has six grandchildren and one great-grandchild. He is now retired and living in Bundaberg, Queensland. He writes and carries his sketch-pad around and along with fishing, he leads a very peaceful and relaxing existence.

Lisa Bellear is Goernpil/Noonuccal of the Quandamooka Nation. She does voluntary broadcasting with 3CR Community Radio in Melbourne where she presents 'Not Another Koori Show'. Lisa is currently completing a PhD (English) at La Trobe University: Contemporary Indigenous issues through radio and photographic texts. Lisa loves dancing, taking photographs and telling bad jokes. And if people must know, she was born May 2 1960.

John Muk Muk Burke is a Wiradjuri man from Narrandera, New South Wales. He has published numerous articles, poems and a novel. His *Night Song and Other Poems* (NTU Press) won the RAKA Awards in 2000. *Bridge of Triangles*, a novel, won the David Unaipon Award in 1993 (UQP, 1994). Muk Muk lives in Darwin.

Graeme Dixon was born in 1955 to a noongah mother and wajella migrant father. He and his six siblings spent much of their childhood in children's institutions; Graeme was in a juvenile institution by the age of fourteen and in maximum-security prison from age sixteen to twenty-five. In the following ten years he lived on the streets, his life dominated by drugs and alcohol.

It was in 1988 while he was detoxing in Royal Perth Hospital that a friend entered writings he'd done while in prison and on the streets in the inaugural David Unaipon Award for Aboriginal writers. Graeme won first prize — $2000 and a publishing contract — and as a result returned to study. He now makes his living as a lecturer and writer.

Josie Douglas is of Wardaman descent — her grandmother's country is just south of Katherine in the Northern Territory. Josie commissioned the anthology *Message Stick: Contemporary Aboriginal Writing* and, with Kateri Akiwenzie-Damm, compiled the international anthology of Indigenous writing, *Skins*, both for IAD Press. Josie has also worked on a wide range of fiction, trade and academic titles and in 2000 became Publisher at IAD Press, the first Aboriginal person to achieve such a position. She has a Bachelor of Arts (Australian Studies) from the University of South Australia and currently lives in Alice Springs with her partner and children.

Jim Everett was born on Flinders Island in 1942, leaving primary school at the age of fourteen years. Jim began writing poetry at age six, and later was influenced by Jack Davis' play *The Dreamers* to write his first play, entitled *We Are Survivors*.

Jim has spent thirteen years of his life at sea on fishing boats, traders and oil tankers. He completed four years in the regular army before travelling around Australia during the

1960s, finally returning to Tasmania and joining in the political struggle during the 1980s and '90s. Jim has been published in many anthologies, has written a number of plays, and has been involved in quite a few film productions. He currently works as a cultural consultant from his home on Cape Barren Island on the north-east coast of Tasmania.

Richard Frankland was born in 1963 and is of Gunditjmara descent. He is an award-winning writer and director of short films, most notably *Harry's War* and *No Way to Forget*. In 1996 *No Way to Forget* was invited to be screened at the 49th Cannes International Film Festival. The film also won two Australian Film Institute (AFI) awards including Best Short Film, the first film by an Indigenous director to win an AFI award. In March 2000, *Harry's War* won the Hollywood Black Film Festival Jury Prize at the Film Festival Prize in Hollywood. As well as making a name as one of Australia's leading independent film makers, Richard is a talented musician, songwriter, theatre director and writer.

Mary Graham was born in Brisbane and grew up on the Gold Coast. She is a Kombu-merri person and is also affiliated with the Waka Waka group through her mother.

She has lectured and tutored on subjects in Aboriginal history, politics, and comparative philosophy at the University of Queensland and at other educational institutions around the country. She has been on the boards and committees of Aboriginal organisations in Brisbane for many years. Mary has also worked in the consulting environment since 1980, focusing recently on Aboriginal economic development and Aboriginal community development.

Mary was a member of the Council for Aboriginal Reconciliation during its first term and was a member of the

ATSIC Regional Council for South East Queensland for six years. Other activities have included freelance editing and script development work for film and television with Murri-image Production.

She currently does native title research work for the Foundation for Aboriginal and Islander Research Action (FAIRA).

Dr Anita Heiss (Wiradjuri nation) is the author of three books: the historical fiction, *Who Am I? The Diary of Mary Talence* (2001), a poetry collection, *Token Koori* (1998), and the satirical social commentary *Sacred Cows* (1996). Anita has been published widely in Australia and Canada and completed her doctoral thesis on publishing Aboriginal writing in 2001. She is the Deputy Chair of the Australian Society of Authors and works at improving the profile and rights of Indigenous authors.

sammy howard's Aboriginal name, given to him by his aunties, is nennerpertenner (kangaroo). sammy was born in 1953 in northern Tasmania. He started to write his thoughts on paper when he turned forty as a way of expressing his frustration at life's lot. sammy has completed a Bachelor of Arts and a Masters in Fine Art and Design. Creating, whether it be in clay or on paper, will always be part of sammy's life as he believes that they are the most powerful mediums to use when expressing one's beliefs.

Terri Janke was born in Cairns, a descendant of Cape York and Torres Strait Islander peoples — Yadukanu and Meriam peoples.

Terri is a lawyer who has written many articles and reports on legal issues, however she is only now beginning to publish her creative expressions via short stories, novels and poetry. One of Terri's short stories has been selected for the forthcoming *Cadigal Voices*, edited by Anita Heiss.

In 2000 Terri was selected by the Australian Society of Authors to undertake the ASA Mentorship Program. She is working towards the writing of her first novel.

Dr Ruby Langford Ginibi was born in 1934 on Box Ridge Mission, Coraki. She was raised in Bonalbo, forty-eight miles inland from Casino. She went to second form in high school in 1947–8 at Casino, her only formal education ever. In 1949 she moved to Sydney where she went into the rag trade and became a trouser machinist at Brachs clothing factory in Surry Hills.

Ruby is the mother of nine children, who she raised mostly by herself. She lived for eleven years near Coonabarabran, living in tents, or tin shacks, and working at ring-barking, burning-off, lopping, and pegging roo skins. She gravitated between Redfern, and the bush, and Sydney.

Ruby is the grandmother of twenty-one children and the great-grandmother of four children. She is the author of *Don't take your love to town* (1988), *Real Deadly* (1992), *My Bundjalung People* (1994) and *Haunted by the Past* (1999) and a lecturer on Aboriginal history, culture and politics.

Kenny Laughton was born in 1950 and has tribal affiliations with the Eastern Arrernte people of Central Australia. He joined the army in 1968 and served in Vietnam, returning to Central Australia on his discharge in 1971. Between 1991 and 1996 he served successively as director of a number of Aboriginal organisations in Alice Springs, despite the gradual deterioration of his health due to war-related illnesses and injuries. Late in 1996 he was assessed as TPI (Totally and Permanently Incapacitated) and awarded a pension by the

Department of Veterans' Affairs. Since his enforced retirement, Kenny has been writing. Co-author of *The Aboriginal Ex-servicemen of Central Australia*, he ventured towards fiction — or faction — for the first time with *Not Quite Men, no longer boys*. He is currently working on *Finders Keepers*, an epic novel based in the Central Australian goldfields.

Melissa Lucashenko, born in 1967, is a Murri woman of mixed European and Yugambeh/Bundjalung descent, and has affiliations with the Arrernte and Waanyi peoples. Melissa worked in blue collar jobs including martial arts instruction and bar work before attending Griffith University, where she received an honours degree in politics. Her first novel, *Steam Pigs*, won the 1998 Dobbie Award for Australian women's fiction and was shortlisted for the NSW Premier's Literary Award. *Killing Darcy*, a young adult novel, won the Royal Blind Society Award for Young Adult Talking Books in 1999. Melissa's third book *Hard Yards* was released in 1999.

June Mills was born in Darwin and comes from a well known Larrakia family. June is a multi-skilled artist, well known for her singing with her sisters, the Mills Sisters. She has been writing and performing publicly since the '70s and as a solo artist for the last ten years. Many of her live performances use the full spectrum of her artistic skills, including visual arts, play writing, poetry, politics and theatrical performance. June also takes an active role in Aboriginal affairs and regional politics and is well known for her unique comedy as well as her beautiful singing voice.

Romaine Moreton graduated from the Australian Film Television and Radio School with a Master of Arts

Scriptwriting and continues to write for film. She also has a BA in Communications from the University of Technology, Sydney. Romaine is an Indigenous poet who has been writing for ten years, and performing spoken word poetry for the last five years. Romaine has self published a single anthology of poetry called *The Callused Stick of Wanting* which was later published by Magabala Books. She has also performed her poetry at festivals across Australia, including the Festival of the Dreaming, and at venues such as the Sydney Opera House. A half-hour documentary on her poetry and life called *A Walk with Words* was screened on the ABC in 2000.

Bruce Pascoe was born in Richmond, Victoria in 1947. He graduated as a secondary teacher but has also worked as a farmer, fisherman and barman. He now runs Pascoe Publishing with his wife, Lyn. Until recently, they also published the successful quarterly, *Australian Short Stories*. He has two children and lives at Cape Otway in Victoria where he is a member of the Wathaurong Aboriginal Co-operative. His books include *Night Animals* (1986), *Fox* (1988), *Ruby-eyed Coucal* (1996), *Shark* (1999, winner of the Fellowship of Australian Writers' Literature Award) and *Nightjar* (2000).

Rosemary Plummer is Warumungu and comes from Tennant Creek in the Northern Territory. In 2000, writing under the pen name Ama, she took out the Aboriginal and Torres Strait Islander Award as part of the Northern Territory University Literary Awards with 'Napanangka Has Gone Digging for Sand Frogs'. She had been highly commended in previous years for her poems.

Recently Rosemary was employed as Project Officer for Barkly Regional Arts in Tennant Creek. She has been collecting stories from old people around Tennant Creek and is hoping to publish them one day.

Boori Monty Pryor is Kunggandji and Birri-gubba from North Queensland and was born in Townsville in 1950. Boori travels extensively as a performer and public speaker throughout Australia and overseas and, with Meme McDonald, has written three books. *Maybe Tomorrow* (Penguin) received a special commendation at the 1998 Human Rights Awards and was shortlisted in the Children's Book Council Awards 1999. *My Girragundji* (Allen & Unwin) won the Children's Book Council Book of the Year for Younger Readers 1999. *The Binna Binna Man* (Allen & Unwin) won three awards at the NSW State Literary Awards 2000 and Boori's narration won the Author/Narrator and Book of the Year awards at the Australian Audio Awards.

Kerry Reed-Gilbert is a Wiradjuri woman from central New South Wales. Kerry began concentrating on her writing several years ago and believes that her writing allows her to be true to her personal totem, the white cockatoo, which in her language means messenger. Kerry draws on her experience and knowledge from being just one member of a large extended Koori family. She is the youngest of eight, the second eldest of six and stuck somewhere in twelve, that's her mob.

Kerry's photography has been exhibited in numerous exhibitions and published in books, catalogues and magazines.

Her first poetry book titled *Black Woman, Black Life* was published by Wakefield Press. In 1997 she compiled and edited *Message Stick* for IAD Press. She also compiled and edited *The Strength of Us as Women: Black Women Speak*, published by Ginninderra Press.

Peter Stevens (Ngimaliny), a Guruma elder, was born at Hamersley Station in the Pilbara region of north-west Australia in 1927. The old people, who taught him their songs, stories and customs, raised him in the traditional way. At the age of fourteen he started work as a stockman and worked either on stations or as a railway employee until his retirement in 1989. As one of the few surviving speakers of the Guruma language his time is now spent as a teacher, spokesperson and custodian of Guruma lands and making a variety of wooden artefacts that are sought after worldwide.

Nelson Hughes (Borliwaynbangu), a Guruma elder, was born on Brockman station in the Pilbara region of north-west Australia in 1923. He spent all his life on Hamersley Station until his retirement in 1984. His first job, at about thirteen years old, was mustering sheep on horseback, and then he worked as the windmill man's assistant. He also assisted the mechanic with maintenance and repairs to station machinery and worked his way up to be the station mechanic and head stockman. His eleven children were all raised on Hamersley Station and all went away to school. Nelson now divides his time between his family and his role as spokesperson and custodian of Guruma country.

Bindimayi (Baldy) was a Guruma man whose songs were made before Peter and Nelson's time. He and one of his brothers were the only song makers at that time. The old people passed down his songs to Peter and Nelson. He was Peter's uncle and Nelson's grandmother's brother and is buried in the bush in the Ashburton region.

Alf Taylor was born in Perth in the late 1940s. He spent his early years with his family in Perth, but later joined his brother Ben at New Norcia Mission. Alf spent many years there, none of which he regards too fondly. When he was able to leave, he ran and, as a young man, spent many years working as a seasonal farm worker in and around Geraldton and Perth. Alf later was able to join the armed forces and was stationed at various locations around Australia. After leaving, he went back home. He was married, but is now divorced, produced seven children (only two of whom survive) and then found his feet as a writer, poet and latter-day black saint to the homeless.

Pat Mamanyjun Torres is a writer, artist and storyteller from the Jugun and Julbayi clans of Yawuru, and the Jabirr-Jabirr and Nyul-Nyul groups of the West Kimberley region of Western Australia, near Broome.

Her two books, *The Story of Crow* and *Jalygurr, Aussie Animal Rhymes* were published in 1987. She also illustrated the highly acclaimed *Do Not Go Around the Edges*, written by Daisy Utemorrah, which won the Australian Multicultural Children's Literature Award. During 1991 she was awarded a Special Commendation Human Rights Award. During 1994 Pat received an Honors Award from the International Board on Books for Young People (IBBY) for her illustrations in *Do Not Go Around the Edges*.

Pat has travelled extensively overseas in the last ten years as an Indigenous storyteller and performer and is currently living in Perth where she is lecturer and unit co-ordinator at the Centre for Aboriginal Studies, Curtin University of Technology. Pat has a Bachelor of Arts and a Graduate Diploma of Education (Primary) and has spent more than twenty years working in Aboriginal education and community development.

Samuel Wagan Watson was born in Brisbane in 1972. He started writing poetry whilst working in the local film and television industry in 1995. In that year his verse was first published in literary magazines, including *Overland*, *Imago* and *Southerly*. It was also his first taste of the performance poetry scene, with a debut reading for the Brisbane Fringe Festival.

In 1999, his first collection of poetry, *of muse, meandering and midnight* (now published by UQP) won the David Unaipon Award and has gone on to win Highly Commended accolades in the 2000 Anne Elder Poetry Award and the 2000 Centre for Australian Cultural Studies Award. His second collection, *itinerant blues*, also with UQP, will be available in early 2002. In 2001, he also wrote a collection for Vagabond Press, titled *hotel bone*, which was launched in Sydney in May.

He is now working on a fourth collection, *darkness and sirens* and a young adult fiction verse novel, *dead on arrival*, set in modern West End concerning the activities of a coven of weredingo.

Brenda Webb is a multi-talented artist. Her solo exhibition 'No Place For Arachnophobes' included her paintings as part of the 2001 NAIDOC celebrations at the Parramatta Riverside Theatre; her acting credits include *Radiance* with the New England Theatre Company and television appearances on 'Neighbours' and 'A Country Practice'; she is a singer and songwriter and has also done radio plays, short films, videos, musicals, documentaries and modelling along with her poetry and other writing.

She recently completed a book of poetry titled *Nubu* (Bundjalung — Tomorrow; Yesterday) and hopes to have it published.